WISDOM TREE

Contents

1. **Peace** — 3
   Peace begins with a smile

2. **Speak the Truth Always** — 10
   A true friend will always speak the truth no matter what

3. **Hygienic Living** — 14
   Health is wealth

4. **Helpfulness** — 22
   A friend in need is a friend indeed

5. **Forgiveness** — 30
   Forgiving is greater than taking revenge

6. **Know the Good from the Bad** — 35
   All that glitters is not gold

7. **Duty** — 42
   What needs to be done has to be done

Peace

Peace means not having a war; not fighting with others. Peace also means being friendly with others. We also spread peace when we willingly share with others. The world is more beautiful when there is peace all around. Fighting is not good for anyone. Peace is good for everyone.

Let us understand more about peace from the story below.

Sameer walked into the playground. All his friends were in the field playing football.

He joined one of the teams and kicked the ball with all his strength. He was trying to make a goal for his team.

After a short while, a group of older boys walked into the ground. Sam was one of them. Sam said, "All you little kids, clear the ground. We want to play here."

Sameer and his friends wanted to finish their game. They had just started playing in the field.

What do you think will happen?

a. Will Sameer and his friends clear the ground because they are afraid of the older boys?

b. Will Sam and his friends hurt the little kids if they do not clear the ground?

c. Will Sam and his friends go away because the little kids are not getting off the ground?

Read to know what happened.

Some of Sameer's friends were scared.

"What should we do?" one of them asked.

"Sam and his friends are stronger than us. We should listen to them and go away. We should let them play or they might hurt us," another said.

"But this is not fair, we came here first," another said.

Then Sameer said, "Let us tell them politely that we want to finish our game. Once we finish the game, let us get off the ground so that they can play." Everyone liked this plan.

They went up to the older children and said the same thing.

Sam thought for a while and replied, "That sounds good, Sameer. Once you finish your game, we can start ours. We can share the ground. We don't have to fight over it."

The children came to a peaceful solution. They took turns to play on the ground.

> Isn't this a nice way of solving a problem? It is a peaceful solution. Nobody felt scared or cheated. Nobody fought over the problem.

Have you understood the story? Then answer the questions.

1. What were Sameer and his friends playing? _____
2. Was Sam a part of Sameer's team? _____
3. Why were the little children scared of the older children?
    a. because the older children looked scary.
    b. because the older children were stronger than them.
4. What did Sameer suggest?
    Sameer suggested that the children
    a. take turns in playing on the ground.
    b. have a toss to decide who plays first on the ground.
5. Did the older children agree to Sameer's suggestion? _____
6. Why was their solution a peaceful one?

_____
_____
_____

More about the Value

When you are peaceful, you are happy. When everyone is peaceful, there will be no destruction. People will be safe.

Gandhiji, who is regarded as the Father of the Indian nation, was a peaceful person. He did not like wars. He showed Indians how to get freedom from the British without a war.

5

Let Us Do

1. **Which of these children show peaceful behaviour. Tick or cross the boxes appropriately.**

   a. Ryan makes others listen to him by shouting and threatening them.

   b. When someone doesn't listen to Ronny, he breaks the toys around him.

   c. When her parents are talking to each other, Simmi waits for them to finish talking before saying what she wants to say. She does not talk in between or cry for them to listen to her.

   d. Danish loves to play video games where there are lots of car crashes.

   e. Tina never fights with any of her friends. If she does not like what someone does, she tells them about it sweetly but never fights with them.

2. **Every time you get angry, put a red circle in the box here. Count the number of circles you have in your box.**

Remember that you use more energy to frown (a face that you make when you are angry) than to smile. Instead of wasting your energy in frowning, you can use it for something better.

3. The entire class can sit in a circle. Hold the hands of the persons sitting on either side of you. Close your eyes and remain silent for a minute.

   Meditation makes you a peaceful person.

1. John hit Mohit. Should Mohit

   a. hit John back? Yes No

   b. tell John that it is wrong to hit others? Yes No

2. Maya stepped on Giya's toy. The toy broke. Should Maya

   a. walk away while Giya is crying for her broken toy? Yes No

   b. say 'sorry' and try to fix the broken toy? Yes No

7

Are You a Peaceful Person?

1. If someone pushes you, will you

    a. push them back?

    b. tell them that what they did was not good?

2. If your mother does not make your favourite snack, will you

    a. get angry and refuse to eat the snack that she made?

    b. request her to make it the next day?

3. Do you like to play

    a. video games which involve wars and car crashes?

    b. outdoor games?

If your answers were 'b' for all three questions, you are a peaceful person.

My Peace Pledge:

Place your right hand on your heart and repeat the pledge below.

Peace starts with me.

I will not be angry

I will not shout at people or animals

I will not harm anyone

I will be friendly with all

I will be a peaceful person.

8

Tips to Parents/Teachers

Teach children to listen to others without interrupting. When they listen, they understand. When they understand, they can be more compassionate and peaceful.

Dos and Don'ts

a. Smile. It shows that you are happy and peaceful.
b. Be kind to others.
c. Behave with others the way you like them to behave with you.
d. Never pick a quarrel. Talk and come to a peaceful solution.

A VALUE FOR ME
Peace begins with a smile.

Speak the Truth Always

> Truthfulness means speaking the truth. Truthfulness also means not cheating others. We should always speak the truth. Lying will land us in trouble. People will not believe liars. But people will always believe those who speak the truth.

Let us know more about truthfulness from the story below.

In a little village by a forest, there lived a shepherd boy. Every day, he had to take his sheep to graze near the forests.

One day, the villagers heard the shepherd boy shout, "Tiger! Help someone, it's a tiger."

The villagers picked up whatever sticks or axes they could and ran to where the boy was with his sheep. When they reached there, they saw the boy rolling on the ground with laughter. The villagers were puzzled. They asked him, "Where is the tiger? Did it take away any of the sheep?"

The boy replied, "I was bored, so I decided to play a prank. How you all got fooled so easily." He continued laughing even as the villagers returned to the village.

Several days later, the villagers once again heard the boy shout, "Help! It really is a tiger this time." They once again picked up their sticks and axes and ran to where the boy was.

Once again, the boy was laughing and the people realized it was a prank. An old man among them said, "You may be having fun little boy, but it is not a good thing to lie. Now even if you speak the truth, no one will believe you."

Many days later, the villagers once again heard the boy shout for help. This time none of them paid any attention to him and continued to do what they were doing.

Sometime later, the boy came home crying. He said, "Why did none of you come to help me? There was a huge tiger. It took away a couple of our sheep. I was very scared."

The villagers saw that the boy was now speaking the truth, but just as the old man had said, no one had believed the boy and so no one had gone to help him.

Have you understood the story? Then answer the questions.

1. Where did the shepherd boy take his sheep to graze?
   _____

2. What animal did the boy say had come near his sheep?
   _____

3. Why did the boy lie?
   _____
   _____

4. How many times did the boy lie?
   _____

5. Why did no one believe him even when he spoke the truth?
   _____
   _____

More about the Value

Speaking the truth may be difficult. Sometimes, you may be scared to speak the truth.

Ronny was playing cricket and he broke the windowpane. When his mother asked him who broke it, he owned up and said it was him.

It was difficult for Ronny to speak the truth, but he did it.

Ronny was at peace because he spoke the truth. He was relieved that his mother knew how the windowpane broke. His mother was upset that the windowpane broke but she was also glad that her son spoke the truth.

A VALUE FOR ME
People who speak the truth are brave.

Let Us Do

1. **Which of the following statements are true? Tick or cross out accordingly.**

   a. Speaking the truth is not always easy.

   b. People will respect you when you speak the truth.

   c. You are not brave if you speak the truth.

   d. The opposite of truth is lies.

   e. Lying is bad.

2. **Every time you lie this week, put a cross in the following table. Be honest.**

   At the end of the week, check the box again. Then answer the following:

   a. Are you happy with your behaviour? (Yes/No)

   b. Do you feel good about lying? (Yes/No)

   c. Can you do better and not lie at all? (Yes/No)

3. **Do you remember the last time that you lied? Answer the following:**

   I lied to my _____ that _____

   _____

   _____

   _____.

   I lied because:

   a. I was scared   b. I was jealous

   c. I was angry   d. I liked teasing her/him

What Should They Do?

1. **Mehak tore her friend's book. Should she:**

   a. tell her friend and say 'sorry' ☐

   b. act as if she does not know about the tear in the book ☐

2. **Siddharth does not go to school because he wants to watch cartoons. His friend Peter knows about this. When the teacher asks if anyone knows why Siddharth is absent, should Peter:**

   a. remain silent and act as if he does not know why Siddharth is absent ☐

   b. tell the teacher the truth about Siddharth ☐

Sometimes, when we speak the truth, we might hurt our friends and family. If Peter speaks the truth and tells the teacher that Siddharth stayed back at home to watch cartoons, Siddharth might get angry with Peter. He might stop being friends with Peter.

But then, by speaking the truth, Peter is being a good friend. He and his teacher will now ensure that Siddharth always does what is right and not be absent from school for cartoons or other silly reasons.

Tips to Parents/Teachers

Speak the truth and encourage children to speak the truth. Tell them how much you respect them for telling the truth.

Dos and Don'ts

1. Never lie.
2. Try to speak the truth always.
3. Remaining silent also means lying.
4. Practice makes a man perfect. Practice speaking the truth. It may be difficult in the beginning, but it will soon become a habit.

A VALUE FOR ME
Always speak the truth.

Hygienic Living

We take a bath daily, brush our teeth twice a day and eat fresh food so that we remain healthy. Hygienic living means living with cleanliness and good habits to remain healthy. Hygienic living can keep us free from germs and diseases.

What would you like to be?

a. healthy and strong ☐

b. sick and weak ☐

How would you like to appear?

a. clean and smart ☐

b. dirty and shabby ☐

Let us know more about hygiene from the story below.

The first thing Sid does every morning after waking up is brush his teeth. He loves his teeth clean and sparkling.

He never misses a bath and always dresses in clean, well-washed clothes. He combs his hair and clips his nail properly.

None of his teachers or friends has ever seen him dirty.

His room too is always neat. His mother changes his bedsheets to keep the bed fresh and Sid helps her.

Sid is the perfect example of hygienic living, but he was never always like this. There was one thing that Sid forgot almost every day—washing his hands before eating food.

"Have you washed your hands, Sid?"

"Oops, I forgot mumma."

His forgetfulness landed Sid in deep trouble once.

Some days ago, Sid was at school. Just like every day, he forgot to wash his hands before eating. Earlier that day, Sid had played in the sand pit of the school. During the lunch break, he reached out for his food with his dirty hands.

Later that evening, he was rolling in pain. His stomach was aching and he was vomiting.

Sid was taken to the doctor. The doctor told Sid's mother that Sid had stomach flu. This happens when people do not wash their hands properly before eating. It was very painful. Sid had to take lots of bitter medicines to get well again.

Sid then thought, "If only I had washed my hands before eating!"

So he learnt his lesson the painful way. Next time onwards, he never ever came to the table without washing his hands. Today, Sid is an example of hygienic living.

Have you understood the story? Then answer the questions.

1. What is the first thing that Sid does after waking up every morning?
   _____
   _____
   _____

2. What are some of the other good things that Sid does to be hygienic?
   _____
   _____
   _____

3. Was Sid always an example of hygienic living?
   _____
   _____
   _____

4. What did Sid always forget to do before eating?
   _____
   _____
   _____

5. What did this forgetfulness lead to? What did Sid suffer from?
   _____
   _____
   _____

More about the Value

Simple habits like washing our hands before eating, keeping our nails clipped, washing fruits and vegetables before cooking them, eating from clean plates, drinking boiled or treated water and so on will keep us healthy.

It is better to have good habits and not fall sick rather than fall sick and then take bitter medicines to get well again.

Let Us Do

1. Which of the following children show an example for hygienic living? Tick or cross the pictures accordingly.

2. Hygienic living begins with cleanliness. Write how you can be clean and keep your surroundings clean.

a. _____

b. _____

c. _____

d. _____

e. _____

3. Write a few lines about 'Swachh Bharat Abhiyaan'. Also, paste pictures.

Swachh Bharat Abhiyaan

_____

_____

_____

_____

_____

What Should They Do?

1. Gia plucked some guavas from the tree. She wants to eat them. But first she should: _____ them. (Wash/Cut)

2. Amit is eating peanuts while in the car. After finishing the peanuts in the packet, he wants to throw the packet away. He should:

    a. do so immediately

b. wait to see a dustbin and then throw the empty packet in the dustbin

3. Monika drinks a glass of sweet milk every night before sleeping. After drinking milk, she should:

   a. sleep immediately
   b. brush her teeth and then sleep

Are You a Hygienic Person?

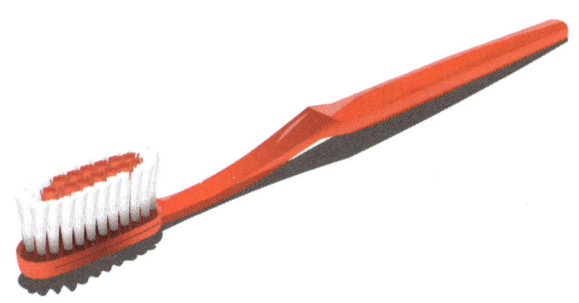

1. Do you brush your teeth every day?

   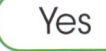

3. Do you take a bath every day?

2. Do you comb your hair every day?

4. Do you wash your hands before and after eating?

   Yes   No

5. Do you put waste only in the dustbin?

 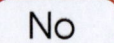

6. Do you eat fresh fruits every day?

7. Do you eat a balanced diet—rice or chapatis, pulses and vegetables every day?

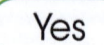 

8. Do you drink milk every day?

If your answer to all the above is 'yes', then you are a hygienic person.

Tips to Parents/Teachers

Encourage children to be hygienic. Make them responsible for keeping their belongings and their room clean. Remind them to wash their hands and brush their teeth.

Dos and Don'ts

Put the following in the correct column.

Don't wash your hands before eating food.	Junk food is good for your health.
Brush your teeth twice a day.	Keep your surroundings clean.
Eat roadside food. It is very healthy.	Wear clean clothes after your bath.

Drink plenty of water every day.	Drink water which is not fresh.
Throw waste out of your windows.	Always eat healthy food.
Wash fruits and vegetables before cooking/eating.	Wash your hands with soap before eating.
Wear the same clothes every day without washing them.	Do not rinse your mouth after eating food.

Dos	Don'ts

A VALUE FOR ME
Health is wealth.

Helpfulness

When you bring in the morning paper from the doorstep and give it to your parents, you are being helpful. When you give a pencil to your friend who forgot to get hers, you are being helpful. When you offer to dust the TV cabinet for your parents, you are being helpful.

Helpfulness is a good quality to have. When you are helpful, you feel good. The people whom you help also feel good. You make friends when you are helpful.

Let us know more about being helpful from the story below.

Have you wondered why ants move in a line? Have you seen where they take the food that they carry on their back? Have you thought of why ants are never alone? If you find one ant on your bed, there are many more to follow.

A group of ants is known as a 'colony'. This is because ants live in large groups. They always help each other.

If one of the ants finds food, it signals to the other ants from its colony. A few ants come over to where the food is. Together, they carry the food back to their anthill.

Ants always help each other. Some ants are called worker ants. Their job is to collect food. They collect as much food as they can throughout summer.

Other ants in the colony are called soldier ants. It is their job to protect the anthill and the ants belonging to their colony.

When winter arrives, all these ants settle back in their anthill and eat from the food they had collected.

An ant can carry loads 50 times its weight. Imagine how much food they can carry into their hills when they all work together!

We can also learn to be helpful. Just like the ants, if we all do our own work and then help others near us, we can all be happy.

But remember, you first need to do your own work before helping others.

Have you understood the message? Then solve the crossword by answering the following questions.

1. Worker ants help the colony by _____ food.
2. No ant _____ for itself. It _____ for the entire colony. (same word)
3. _____ ants help the colony by protecting the other ants.
4. We should all be _____ to each other.
5. Ants live in large groups called _____.

More about the Value

Have you ever been in an aircraft? The air hostess tells us that in case the oxygen masks drop to the seats, we have to put on our own masks first before helping others around us.

Sometimes in class, those children who finish their work first, help others complete theirs, with the teacher's permission.

At home, after finishing your homework, don't we all help our parents do some household work?

When you are helpful:

   a. people whom you have helped feel happy

   b. you also feel happy

Let Us Do

1. **Many people help us every day. For instance, the tailor helps us by stitching or mending our clothes. Can you name some other people who help us? Paste pictures too.**

1.	2.
3.	4.
5.	6.
7.	8.

2. **Have you ever helped anyone? Describe how you have helped them.**

   a. (your parents) _____
   _____
   _____
   _____
   _____
   _____
   _____
   _____

   b. (your friend) _____
   _____
   _____
   _____
   _____
   _____
   _____
   _____

   c. (a stranger) _____
   _____
   _____
   _____
   _____
   _____
   _____
   _____

3. Paste pictures of people helping others.

What Should They Do?

1. Danish does not know how to finish his art and craft project. Should his friend Kalpana:

   a. help Danish by telling him how to do it

   (Sometimes, it is not good to help. Here Danish should learn the answers by himself.)

2. Archie is walking back home. He sees his elderly neighbour carrying a basket. She is also going home. Should Archie:

   a. greet her and go ahead

   b. greet her and offer to help her carry the basket to her house

Mock Situation

You are running a race. Your friend falls down and gets hurt. What will you do? Will you continue to run the race? Will you stop running and help your friend? Discuss in class.

Tips to Parents/Teachers

These are some of the things you can get children to do at home.

- Clean bedroom
- Dust furniture
- Feed the family pet
- Help care for or play with a younger sibling
- Help fold laundry
- Help set the table
- Help clean the garden
- Pick up toys
- Put away groceries
- Put clean clothing inside wardrobes
- Put dirty clothes in the wash basket
- Put dirty dishes in the kitchen sink
- Sweep or vacuum
- Water plants
- Wipe up messes

Dos and Don'ts

1. Help as many people as you can.
2. You need not know the person to help them. For example, you can help a younger child, whom you do not know, to cross the road.
3. Never help anyone do something wrong.
4. When someone helps you, always say, "Thank you."
5. When someone thanks you for your help, you say, "It wasn't a problem," or "It was my pleasure."

A VALUE FOR ME
A friend in need is a friend indeed.

Forgiveness

When you are upset with your friend, do you stop being his or her friend? Or, do you become friends again after some time?

You become friends again because you have forgiven each other.

We should learn to forgive people. It will make us happier, and win back our friends.

Let us know more about forgiveness from the story below.

Have you heard of the lion that forgave the mouse?

Once, there was a lion that was sleeping in its den. It was tired after a long hunt and a good meal. All it wanted was to rest peacefully.

A mouse that lived near the den was not that lucky. It was still hungry. The mouse was searching for leftovers in the den.

It unfortunately stepped on the sleeping lion's tail. The lion woke up with a loud roar. "Who dare disturb my sleep?" he asked angrily.

The mouse trembled with fear. When the lion saw that it was the mouse that disturbed its sleep, it lifted its paw to squash the mouse.

"Please forgive me," said the mouse. "I am small and weak. I was searching for food. Please forgive me," it pleaded.

The lion took pity on the mouse and forgave it.

Many days later, the same lion was caught in a hunter's net. It could not escape. The mouse saw the lion trapped in the net. It went ahead and nibbled away at the net, setting the lion free.

The lion thanked the mouse and ran away into the jungle.

The lion realized that day that by forgiving, it had won a loyal friend.

Have you understood the story? Then answer the questions.

1. The _____ was sleeping in its den.   (lion/mouse)

2. The _____ stepped on the _____'s tail.   (lion/mouse)

3. The mouse begged for _____.   (a hunt/forgiveness)

4. The _____ saved the _____ from the hunter's net.   (lion/mouse)

5. By forgiving, the lion had won a loyal _____. (friend/hunter)

More about the Value

Forgiving someone is not very easy. When someone hurts you, you feel like hurting them back too. But, by doing so, you will not be any different from them. Just because someone has hurt you, it does not mean that you should hurt them too.

Rather, you should go to them and tell them how you were hurt by them. You should then tell them that you forgive them.

Let Us Do

1. **Say true or false.**

   a. Soham does not like Raghu. When Raghu fell off his cycle, Soham felt happy. Soham is a forgiving person.

   True　False

   b. Lisa and Julie had a fight. They became friends once again after some time. They are both forgiving persons.

   True　False

   c. Mike pushed Jim. Jim no longer talks to Mike. Jim is a forgiving person.

   True　False

2. Are you angry with someone? Write down why you are angry with that person. Let us not name that person. We will call him or her XYZ.

   Now think of something nice about that person. Think of when that person helped you, or was kind to you. Write it down in the next column. Whenever you feel upset with that person, remember the good thing about them. This way you will be able to forgive that person easily.

I am angry with XYZ because

_____
_____
_____
_____
_____

I like XYZ because

_____
_____
_____
_____
_____

3. What do we feel when we forgive? Circle the correct words.

Happy   Kind   Angry   Sleepy   Peaceful   Bad

Hungry   Friendly   Jealous   Scared   Nice

What Should They Do?

Tick the correct answer.

1. It was Koel's birthday party. She forgot to invite her friend Samaira.

   a. Should Koel say 'sorry'?
   b. Should Samaira forgive Koel?

33

2. **Mike is a naughty boy. He splashed paint on Ada's shirt. Should Ada:**

   a. put some paint on Mike?

   b. inform her teacher about what Mike did?

   c. forgive Mike and continue with her work?

It is okay to forgive someone when they did something by mistake. It is okay to forgive someone when they apologize. But when people like Mike are naughty, we should inform the teacher or some elder. That way, we will make sure that the elder person will correct Mike's misbehaviour.

Is Shreya a forgiving person?

She is not really forgiving. When you forgive a person, you should be ready to forget what the other person has done.

Tips to Parents and Teachers

Before a child forgives someone, it is important for them to know the emotion they are going through. It also works the other way round. When a child asks to be forgiven, he or she should understand what wrong they had done, for which they are asking forgiveness.

Help children realize the emotion for which they are forgiving or asking to be forgiven.

Dos and Don'ts

1. Apologize when you have done something wrong.
2. When someone apologizes, forgive them.
3. If you don't like what someone has done, tell them so.
4. If someone hurts you, you don't have to hurt them back.

A VALUE FOR ME
Forgiving is greater than taking revenge.

Know the Good from the Bad

Do you know what is good for you and what is bad? Since you are young, your parents tell you to finish your homework before playtime because it is good for you. They also tell you not to stay up late because it is not good for you.

As you grow up, you should know for yourself what is good for you and what is not.

Let us know more about this from the incidents below.

Ricky's Good Decision

The ice cream shop was round the corner. Ricky was tempted. He loved ice creams and he wanted to eat them right now.

But then, Ricky had a cold. He was sneezing and coughing. He was returning from the doctor. The doctor had told him to rest well and keep himself warm.

When Ricky saw the ice cream shop, he just passed by it. He did not ask his mother to buy him some of that delicious, cold ice cream. After all, an ice cream could make his cold worse.

Ricky knew what was good for him and what was not.

Shabana's Foolishness

The children were playing in the garden. When Shabana hit the ball, it flew into the air and got stuck in one of the higher branches of a mango tree.

The children were worried. They needed their ball back. Shabana decided to climb the tree to get the ball. Her friend Swati said, "I think it is dangerous Shabana. The ball is stuck in the higher branches. You might fall and hurt yourself."

But Shabana did not listen to her friend. "Don't worry Swati. I can climb trees very well. I will get back our ball in two minutes," she said.

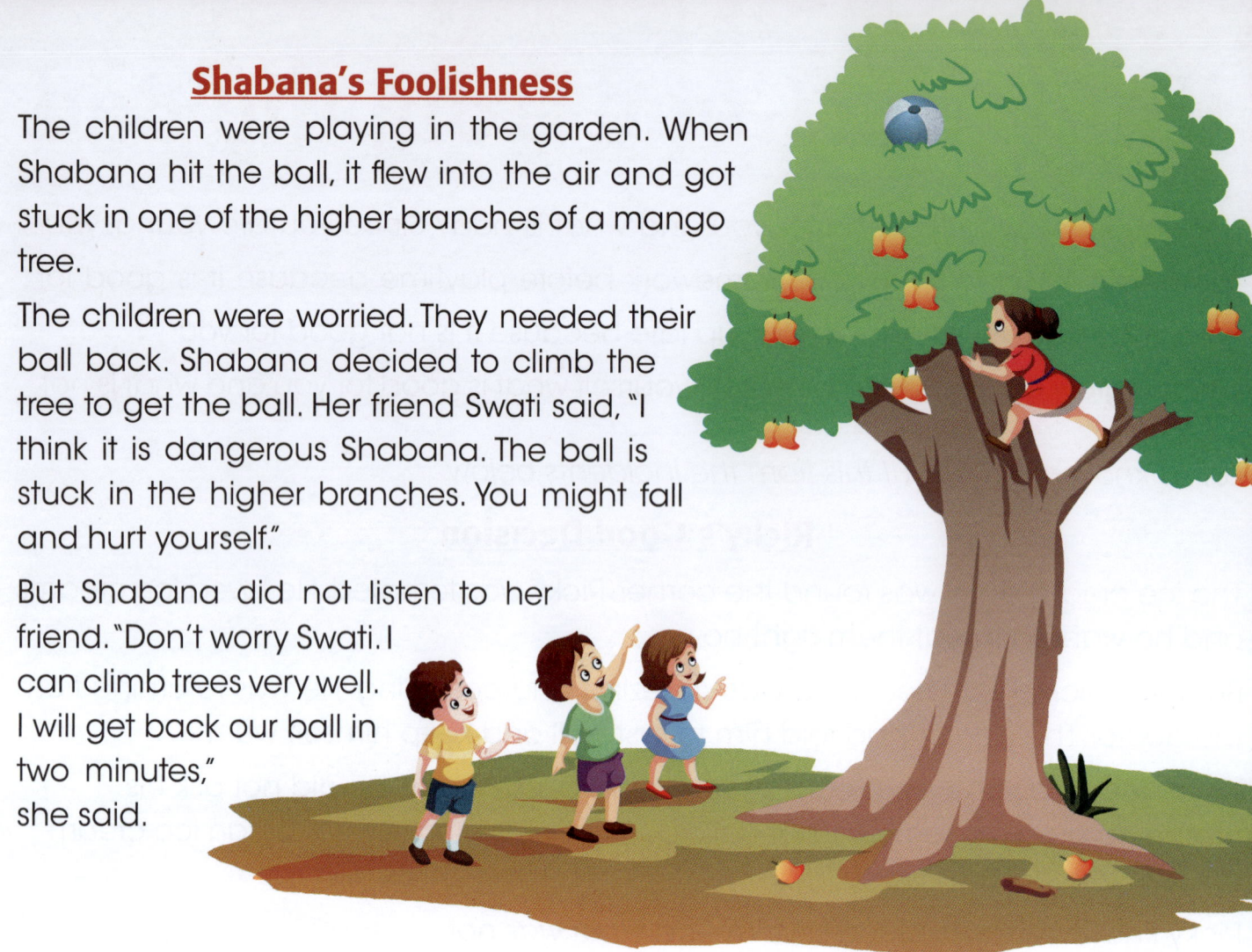

Shabana started climbing the tree. Unfortunately, she slipped and fell to the ground. She hurt her leg badly and could not play for a week after that.

Shabana ought not to have climbed the tree. She should have listened to her friend Swati. To get the ball back, the children should have asked the help of an adult.

Have you understood the stories? Then solve the crossword by answering the questions below.

1. Ricky was tempted to have _____.

2. He did not have it because he had a _____.

3. Shabana climbed the _____ tree to get the ball back.

4. Shabana _____ to the ground and hurt herself.

5. Ricky knew what was _____ for him but Shabana didn't.

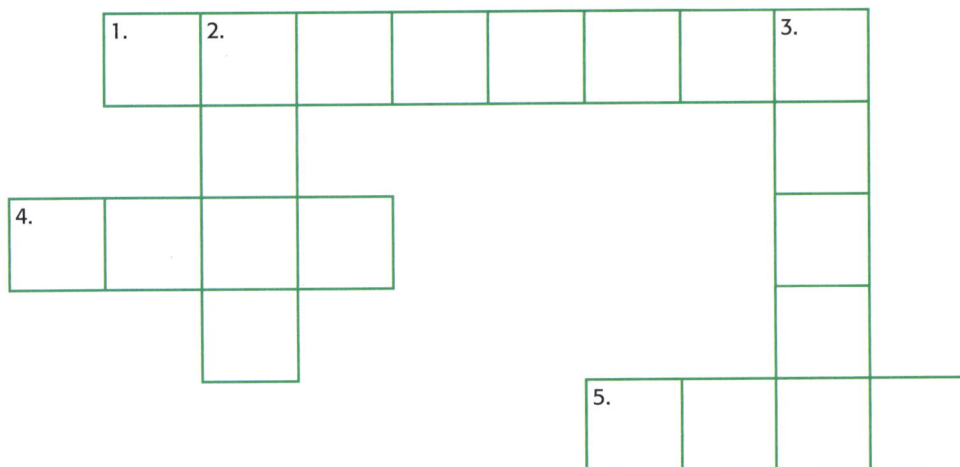

More about the Value

Your teachers and elders tell you what is good and bad for you. You should listen to them carefully. As you grow up, you will be able to tell what is good or bad for you. When you follow what is good, you will grow into a healthy and wise person.

You should also remember that some things are very tempting. To eat a chocolate is more fun that eating green vegetables. But you should remember that green vegetables are really good for your health. Chocolates, on the other hand, can give you cavities.

Let Us Do

1. **Which among the following are good for you and which are bad? Colour the good ones green and the bad ones red.**

   a. Brushing your teeth before sleeping

   b. Eating chocolates every day

   c. Turning off the tap after using it

   d. Sleeping for only five hours

   e. Sharing with friends

   f. Picking a fight in the playground

   g. Playing outdoors in the evening

   h. Sleeping on time

   i. Two glasses of milk every day

   j. Video games

37

2. **Make a list of three good and three bad characters from the cartoons you see. Paste their pictures or draw them. Write in one sentence why they are good and why they are bad.**

38

3. Here is a list of how we all behave at times. Sort them into columns as to whether they are good or bad behaviour.

   Angry   Happy   Jealous   Friendly

   Good: _____   _____

   Bad: _____   _____

   Here are some things that are good for you and some that are bad. Sort them out.

   Exercise   Laziness   Cola Drinks   Fruits

   Good: _____   _____

   Bad: _____   _____

What Should They Do?

1. Vikram is at the traffic signal. The red light is on. There is no other car on the road. Should he:

   a. wait for the light to turn green

   b. drive on because the road is empty

2. **It is raining. Farah is tempted to play in the rain. Should she:**

   a. go ahead and play in the rain

   b. ask her parents first if it is okay to play in the rain

(Sometimes, without realizing it, you could catch a cold or fall sick if you play in rain. It is better to first ask your parents.)

3. **James and his family are at the beach for a picnic. At the end of the picnic, they should:**

a. pick up their belongings and go home

b. pick up their belongings and put away the trash in a dustbin before they leave. If there is no dustbin, they should put all the trash in a bag and throw it in a dustbin on the way back.

Tips to Parents and Teachers

Along with telling children what to do and what not to do, explain to them why it is good or bad to do something. Children should be explained things properly so that they can think for themselves and act accordingly.

Dos and Don'ts

1. Understand what is good or bad for you.
2. Even if you are tempted to do something bad, you should not do it.
3. Doing good things may be very difficult. Show the world that you are a strong person and do what is only good or correct.

A VALUE FOR ME
All that glitters is not gold.

Duty

Everyone has a task that needs to be done. It is the teacher's responsibility to teach children. It is the policeman's responsibility to catch thieves. It is a child's responsibility to listen to his or her elders. All these responsibilities are known as duties. Everyone should perform his or her duty.

Let us know more about duty from the story below.

Shibi was a king who ruled over the Indian state of Kerala many years ago. He was a great king and people were very happy under his rule.

His duty, like any other king's, was to keep his people safe and happy. He did whatever he could to help his people. He always fulfilled his promises.

Once, a pigeon flew to him. It asked the king, "O great king, please promise that you will keep me safe. Promise me that you will not let anything harm me."

The king immediately promised to keep the pigeon safe. As soon as he promised, an eagle flew down to where the king and the pigeon were. When the king saw that the pigeon was scared of the eagle, he said, "Eagle, I have promised to keep the pigeon safe from all harm. Be careful of what you do, for you are scaring him."

The eagle looked at the king and said, "Before the pigeon came to you, I was chasing it. He is my meal, and I was hunting it. Will you not let a poor, hungry eagle hunt and eat its prey?"

The king was now puzzled. He had promised to keep the pigeon safe. So he could not let the eagle eat it. But then, he could not ask the eagle to return home hungry. Both the birds belonged to his kingdom. He had to look after them both.

After thinking for a while, he came to a decision. He said, "Dear birds, it is my duty as the king to keep both of you happy. I promised the little bird safety. Therefore, I will not allow the eagle to eat it. However, I should not let any living thing in my kingdom be hungry. So I will give the eagle my flesh to satisfy its hunger."

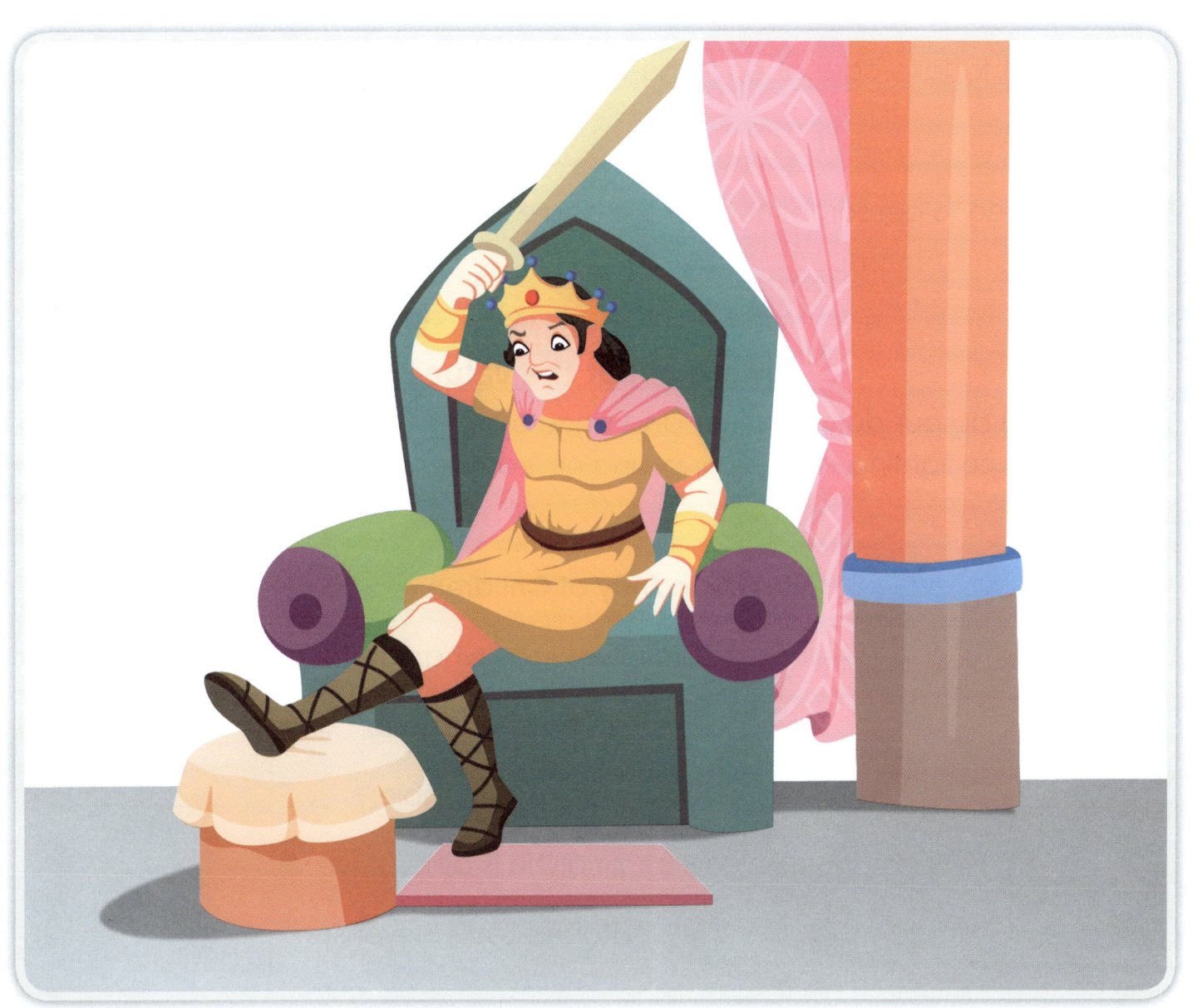

He removed his sword and was about to cut off a part of his thigh to feed the eagle, when both the eagle and the bird turned into gods. They said, "We have always heard of your greatness Shibi, and wanted to see it for ourselves. You sense of duty is great. Please do not cut yourself with the sword."

They blessed the king and went away.

Have you understood the story? Say whether the following are true or false.

1. Shibi was a great king. True / False

2. Shibi offered to keep the eagle from all harm. True / False

3. The eagle was hunting the pigeon. True / False

4. Shibi had to take care of both the birds because they both belonged to his kingdom. True / False

5. Shibi offered to get some meat for the eagle from the palace's kitchens. True / False

More about the Value

When we all do our duty carefully and sincerely, our world will be a better place. There will be no fighting, no cheating, and no war. Everyone will be safe and happy.

Whole Duty of Children

A child should always say what's true

And speak when he is spoken to,

And behave mannerly at table;

At least as far as he is able.

— Robert Louis Stevenson

Let Us Do

1. Are you a dutiful person?

a. Do you listen to your parents?

   Yes   No

b. Do you clean your room by yourself?

   Yes   No

c. Do you do your homework without being told to?

   Yes   No

d. Do you spend time with your grandparents?

   Yes   No

e. Do you help your brother or sister at home?

   Yes   No

If your answers to all the above is yes, you are a dutiful person.

2. Which of the following are our duties? Circle the correct ones.

a. Loving our parents

b. Dirtying our surroundings

c. Loving our country

d. Dirtying our clothes and shoes

e. Being friendly with our neighbours

f. Wasting electricity

g. Wasting food

h. Helping others in whatever way we can

What Should They Do?

1. When the National Anthem is being played, everyone should:

    a. continue doing the work that they are doing

    b. stand up in respect for the country

2. An old man got into the bus. Aryan saw that there were no seats empty. He should:

    a. get up to let the old man sit

    b. continue sitting in his seat

3. Neerja wants to buy a bottle of juice. A lot of people are waiting for their turn at the shop. She should:

    a. also wait for her turn

    b. push herself through everyone and buy the bottle

(Form a queue wherever you can—at the bus stop, the railway station, billing counter at a grocery store, at the ticket counter of a cinema, and so on. That way, those who came first will get their turn first and there will be no pushing or fighting.)

Tips to Parents and Teachers

Point out instances where children can be dutiful. Teach them to be dutiful out of love and respect, and not out of fear.

When duty is done out of love and respect, it is done better.

When it is done out of fear, there are chances that the child will not perform his or her duty when no one is looking.

Dos and Don'ts

Dos	Don'ts
1. Love your parents and grandparents.	1. Never spoil public property like buses and trains by scratching their paint off, or writing on them.
2. Respect your neighbours.	2. Don't waste electricity, water and paper.
3. Love your country.	3. Don't eat junk food and be lazy. It is your duty to take care of your body and health.

A VALUE FOR ME
What needs to be done has to be done.